Inculpatory Evidence
The Covid-19 Poems

หลักฐานเชิงประจักษ์
บทกวี **Covid−19**

SELECTED POETRY BY EILEEN R. TABIOS

After The Egyptians Determined The Shape of the World Is A Circle, 1996
Beyond Life Sentences, 1998
The Empty Flagpole (CD with guest artist Mei-mei Berssenbrugge), 2000
Ecstatic Mutations (with short stories and essays), 2001
Reproductions of The Empty Flagpole, 2002
Menage a Trois With the 21st Century, 2004
The Estrus Gaze(s), 2005
Post Bling Bling, 2005
I Take Thee, English, For My Beloved, 2005
The Secret Lives of Punctuations, Vol. I, 2006
Dredging for Atlantis, 2006
SILENCES: The Autobiography of Loss, 2007
The Light Sang As It Left Your Eyes: Our Autobiography, 2007
Nota Bene Eiswein, 2009
Footnotes to Algebra: Uncollected Poems 1995-2009, 2009
Roman Holiday, 2010
THE THORN ROSARY: Selected Prose Poems and New 1998-2010, 2010
the relational elations   of ORPHANED ALGEBRA (with j/j hastain), 2012
5 Shades of Gray, 2012
THE AWAKENING: A Long Poem Triptych & A Poetics Fragment, 2013
147 Million Orphans (MMXI-MML), 2014
SUN STIGMATA (Sculpture Poems), 2014
I Forgot Light Burns, 2015
Duende in the Alleys, 2015
INVENT(ST)ORY: Selected Catalog Poems & New (1996-2015), 2015
The Connoisseur of Alleys, 2016
The Gilded Age of Kickstarters, 2016
Excavating the Filipino in Me, 2016
I Forgot Ars Poetica, 2016
AMNESIA: Somebody's Memoir, 2016
THE OPPOSITE OF CLAUSTROPHOBIA: Prime's Anti-Autobiography, 2017
To Be An Empire Is To Burn, 2017
If They Hadn't Worn White Hoods ... (with John Bloomberg-Rissman), 2017
What Shivering Monks Comprehend, 2017
IMMIGRANT: Hay(na)ku & Other Poems In A New Land, 2017
Comprehending Mortality (with John Bloomberg-Rissman), 2017
WINTER ON WALL STREET: A Novella-in-Verse, 2017
Making National Poetry Month Great Again, 2017
MANHATTAN: An Archaeology, 2017
Love In A Time of Belligerence, 2017
MURDER DEATH RESURRECTION: A Poetry Generator, 2018
TANKA, Vol. I, 2018
HIRAETH: Tercets From The Last Archipelago, 2018
One, Two, Three: Selected Hay(na)ku Poems (Trans. Rebeka Lembo), 2018
THE GREAT AMERICAN NOVEL: Selected Visual Poetry 2001-2019, 2019
Witness in the Convex Mirror, 2019
Evocare: Selected Tankas (with Ayo Gutierrez and Brian Cain Aene), 2019
The In(ter)vention of the Hay(na)ku: Selected Tercets 1996-2019, 2019
WE ARE IT, 2020

Inculpatory Evidence
The Covid-19 Poems

หลักฐานเชิงประจักษ์
บทกวี Covid–19

Eileen R. Tabios

Thai Translations by Natthaya Thamdee

Afterword by John Bloomberg-Rissman

Laughing/Ouch/Cube/Productions
i.e. press
2020

Copyright © 2020 Eileen R. Tabios
except for
Thai Translations Copyright © 2020 Natthaya Thamdee
Afterword essay "Some thoughts…" Copyright © 2020 John Bloomberg-Rissman
"An N+7 Translation of 'Kapwa on Covid'" Copyright © 2020 Susan M. Schultz

Laughing/Ouch/Cube/Productions
i.e. press
ISBN: 978-1-934299-16-6
Contact: nalandaten@gmail.com and/or johnkathybr@gmail.com

Acknowledgements
These poems have appeared or are forthcoming in the following publications; much gratitude to their editors and publishers:

Covid-19 Diary World Anthology (Editor Christopher Okemwa)
HALIBUT (Editors Susan Gillis and Mary diMichelle)
Materialist: 50th Anniversary of Earth Day E-zine, (Editor Lauren Frick)
MiGoZine (Editor Aileen Cassinetto and Guest Editor Abigail Licad)
Moss Trill (Editor William Allegrezza)
North of Oxford, April 2020 (Editors Diane Sahms and g emil reutter)
Otoliths: A Journal of Many E-Things (Editor Mark Young)
Writing Out of Time (Curator Joseph Harrington)

CONTENTS

Poetics, March 2020 บทกวีเดือนมีนา 2563	3
Regret เสียดาย	7
Triggered ฉุกคิด	9
What I Normally Would Not Buy / Aka Domesticity, 2020 ของที่ปกติไม่ซื้อ / เรียกอีกชื่อหนึ่งว่า ชีวิตแม่บ้าน 2020	13
Not My First Mask aka 2020 Selfie ไม่ใช่มาส์กแรกที่เคยใส่ / หรือเรียกอีกชื่อหนึ่งว่า เซลฟี่ 2020	15
Sudden Asian Prepper เอเชียนผู้ตื่นตระหนก	17
Faith in the Time of the Coronavirus ศรัทธาในภาวะโคโรนา	19
Mortality ความตาย	23
Zucchini Blossom ดอกซูกินี	25
Kapwa On Covid เอกวิญญาณยามโควิด	29
CODA: An N+7 Translation of "Kapwa on Covid" by Susan M. Schultz	31
Behind the Scenes on Translation	35
Afterword by John Bloomberg-Rissman	43
Selected Notes on the Poems	55
About the Poets & Translators	57

POEMS

English with Thai Translations

บทกวีเดือนมีนา 2563

ฉันแต่งบทกวี
มาตลอดชีวิตการเขียนของฉัน
ด้วยภาษาที่กระท่อนกระแท่น สังเวยความโศก

ฉันซ่อนความพังพินาศไว้
ภายใต้ทฤษฎีบทกวี
สนองรบการล่าอาณานิคม

โดยใช้ภาษาอังกฤษมาขูดแทนภาษาแม่
ด้วยเหตุนี้ ฉันจึงชอบใช้ภาษาเกินจริง
มโนคติปะติดถ้อยคำที่พบเจอเข้าด้วยกัน...

เพื่อยืนหยัดอย่างดื้อดึงต่อ
เรื่องราวความทุกข์ที่สร้าง
โดยผู้รุกราน ล่าสุดคือจีน

ผู้ขนเอาดินมากมายหลายคันรถ
อีลุกจากแผ่นดินฟิลิปปินส์
เพื่อไปสร้างเป็นเกาะสำหรับบ่อนพนัน

บนดินแดนกลางมหาสมุทร
ทำให้ปลาเหลือน้อยและสร้างมลพิษ
ด้วยขยะส่งออก (บางที

อาจเพื่อแลกกับการรับเรือ
ขนขยะของโลก
มานานหลายสิบปี)

ในตอนนี้ ขณะที่ไวรัสโคโรนาระบาด
อนุจาเบียร์โคโรนาเสนอเงินกว่า 10 ล้านดอลลาร์
เพื่อขอเปลี่ยนชื่อไวรัสเป็น "บัดไลท์
อีกครั้ง ที่ฉันรู้สึกเสียใจกับพลังของบทกวี
ที่ใช้ทำนาย รับรวมสิ่งปนเปื้อน
ในอากาศเอาไว้ จนกระทั่งสิ้นลม

Poetics, March 2020

To my sorrow, I've been writing poems
the entirety of my writing life
on the collapse of language—

I camouflage my subversions
under theories of poetics
responding to colonialism replacing

my mother tongue with English:
Thus, I fashionably cited surrealism,
abstraction, the collage of found texts…

to remain stubborn against
narrative for the anguish inflicted
by invaders, the latest being China

who literally exports truck loads
of earth from Philippine land
to create false islands for gambling

dens atop an oceanic territory
it stripped of fish and polluted
with exported waste (perhaps

in exchange for decades
of receiving shipping fleets
of the world's garbage)—

Now, as the Corona virus spreads—
poor Corona offering $10 million
to rename it "Bud Light Virus"—

I grieve again over the poem's power
to foretell, to gather what stains
the air until it alchemizes into the clarity

แปรเปลี่ยนเป็นภาพเหตุการณ์ขยาย
ที่จับภาพผ่านเลนส์สะท้อน
ของกล้องขยายภายในใจ

ฉันงอตัว   ในท่าคุดคู้
                                    อยู่บน

ผืนผ้าใหม่ทำจากม้วนกระดาษชำระ
รีดวาจาใด ๆ ดึงขากฎที่ไม่สวมมารถ
สื่อสารได้ มีแค่เพียงน้ำตาที่ไหล

หรือแห้งเหือดไป รูปภาพ
เผยให้เห็นว่าคราบน้ำตาที่จางหาย
มันยะคล้ายทางธารกัดเซาะ

ที่กัดกร่อนโลกมานานนับปี "น่ามหัศจรรย์
ที่ลวดลายของธรรมชาตินั้น
ดูแล้วช่างคล้ายคลึงกัน ต่างกันแค่ขนาด"

จากบันทึกของช่วงภาวะ โรส-ลินน์ ฟิชเชอร์
ควมตรอมใจก่อให้เกิดภาพผลึกแผ่ขยายแบบเดียวกัน
ไม่ว่าจะเกิดจากคราบน้ำตา

ณ ห้วงเวลาหนึ่ง หรือเกิดจากพื้นดินทรุดกร่อน
อย่างไม่หยุดหย่อนตามกาลเวลาที่ไม่หยุดเดิน
"ประหนึ่งน้ำตาแต่ละหยดเป็นโลกย่อส่วน

ของประสบการณ์ที่มนุษย์สั่งสมมา ดั่งหนึ่งหยด
ของมหาสมุทร", ฟิชเชอร์กล่าว หากบทกวีนำเสนอมุมมอง
ของฟิชเชอร์สู่ผู้อ่านเรื่อยไปเช่นนี้

ผ่าน "ศิลปะ," แล้วบทกวีจะไม่ทรงพลังกว่าหรือ
หวกการทำท่าคุดคู้ใด ๆ ของฉันนับเป็นการอุปมา
หรือฉันควรเลิกใช้คำอุปมาพรรณนา ประหนึ่งว่าเพียงภาษาสื่อออกมาได้มากพอ

                              ฉันยังคงอยากรู้
                        แม้ว่าตอนนี้ฉันจะรู้แล้ว
                        ว่าฉันไม่เคยทำได้เลย

of blown-up, detailed scenes
gleaned through the polished lens
of a psychological microscope—

I fold
        into a fetal position
                              against

my new mattress of toilet paper rolls
speechless like a baby who cannot
communicate except for the presence

or absence of tears. Photographs
reveal that the image of a dried tear
shows similar passages of erosion

as have etched earth for years. "Amazing
how the patterns of nature seem so
similar, regardless of scale," notes

the photographer Rose-Lynn Fisher. Anguish
begets the same images of branched crystals
whether from dried tears that formed

in moments or from the consistent deterioration
of a terrain over prolonged passages of time
"As though each tear is a microcosm of

collective human experience, like one drop
of an ocean," says Fisher. If a poet presents
Fisher's observation to you, Reader, unmitigated

by "art," is the poem more effective? Any
fetal position I undertake is metaphorical—
should I forego metaphor as if language suffices?

เสียดาย
-เขียนขึ้นหลังจากที่ได้อ่าน
"ปริมาณการใช้ถุงพลาสติกกลับเพิ่มจำนวนขึ้นเพราะ Covid-19"
โดย Justine Calma จาก The Verge, วันที่ 2 เมษายน 2563

เมื่อถุงพลาสติกกลับมา
แทนที่ถุงผ้าแบบใช้ซ้ำ

เราก็เริ่มได้ยินข่าวแผ่นดินไหว
ตามแนวมหาสมุทรบอยขึ้น

ไม่หรอกน่า แผ่นดินไม่ได้ไหว
เพราะ Covid-19

เมื่อถุงพลาสติกกลับมา
ฝูงปลาก็พากันสนเท่ห์

ความกลัวนั้นทำให้ผืนน้ำปั่นป่วน
ม้วนตลบชายฝั่ง

ด้วยน้ำตาที่ล้นทะลัก
ขอเราจงอย่าลืมว่า ถุงพลาสติก

ที่ลอยเคว้งอยู่กลางมหาสมุทรนั้นต้องใช้เวลา
ย่อยสลายนานกว่า 20 ปี

และขวดน้ำพลาสติก
ที่ลอยเคว้งผลุบ ๆ โผล่ ๆ

ต้องรอไปถึง 450 ปี
จริงอยู่ ก็ยากนะที่จะใส่ใจสิ่งต่าง ๆ

ในเมื่อดูท่าแล้วตัวเราเองก็จะไม่รอด
แต่คงจะดีกว่า หากจะตายไปโดยไม่ต้องเสียดายอะไร

Regret
    —after "Plastic bags are making a comeback because of
    Covid-19"
    by Justine Calma, The Verge, *April 2, 2020*

As plastic bags return
to replace reusable totes,

we hear rising reports of
earthquakes along oceanic beds.

No, Dears, the earth is not
fragmenting over Covid-19.

As plastic bags return
the fish are simply shivering—

their fear roils the water
and overcomes shores with

turbulent tears. Let us
never forget: plastic bags

adrift in the ocean require
up to 20 years to decompose

and a plastic bottle is able to
continue bobbing its emptiness

for up to 450 years. It's hard
to care about matters for

when we ourselves are dead. But,
shall we try dying without regret?

ฉุกคิด
-เมษายน 2563

พ่อกับแม่สอนบทเรียนฉันบทหนึ่ง
ที่คงจะทำให้พวกท่านใจสลาย
และน้ำตาไหลเป็นสายเลือด
อาบรอยเหี่ยวย่นบนใบหน้า
หากพวกท่านได้รู้ว่าฉันไม่เพียงแค่เข้าใจบทเรียนนั้นอย่างถ่องแท้
แต่หายใจรับมันเข้ามาจนกลายเป็นส่วนหนึ่งของตัวฉัน

ความหิวโหย

การเป็นผู้อพยพหมายถึงการต้องหิวโหย
อยู่งตอนที่พ่อลูงโทษตัวเองโดยการยืนต่อแถว
รอรับก้อนเนยแข็งจากรัฐบาล
ที่เป็นสีเหลืองสด
เสียจนคิดว่าอาบด้วยกัมมันตรังสี
แต่ที่แย่สุดก็คือตอนที่ผู้อพยพอิ่มท้อง
เพียงเพื่อจะหิวหา
อยากได้สิ่งที่ซับซ้อนกว่านั้น
จากประเทศใหม่ที่ตนมาอยู่ - การยอมรับ

ผ่านไปปีแล้วปีเล่า ฉันฝ่าฟันใช้ชีวิต
เรียนจนจบมหาวิทยาลัยด้วยเงินเก็บที่พ่อแม่ส่งเสีย
ซึ่งคุ้มครองฉันไปไม่ได้ตลอด ฉันกับสามี
ต้องตื่นมาเจอตู้เย็นที่ว่างเปล่า
หนึ่งวันก่อนเงินค่าจ้างออก
เราโชคดี เราน่าจะได้ใช้
บัตรเครดิตที่เผอิญโชคดีมีให้ใช้
แต่เราระมัดระวังตั้งแต่แรก
ไม่ให้เป็นหนี้บัตรเครดิต เพราะมองว่า
บัตรใบเล็กนั่นเป็นก้าวที่พลาด
บนทางลาดลื่น ๆ
ที่ทำให้เพื่อนผู้หิวโหยของเราพากันล้มทรุดมาแล้ว

เราโชคดียิ่งกว่านั้น ที่เจอทูน่าอีกหนึ่งกระป๋อง
หลบซ่อนอยู่ที่มุมมืดข้างในสุดของตู้กับข้าว
เรารีบเปิดกระป๋องและโรยเกลือ
แล้วใส่มายองเนสทำเป็นมื้อเย็น - สลัดทูน่า!
ถ้าใครมาหาฉันที่บ้าน ฉันคงจะรับรอง

Triggered
       —April 2020

Mom and Dad taught me a lesson
that would break then make their heart
leak from their eyes to run in rivers
matching their facial wrinkles
if they learned I not only understood it
well but inhaled it to become part of me:

hunger.

To be immigrant is to be hungry,
as when Dad punished himself to stand
in line for bricks of government cheese
colored in a yellow so bright it must
have been radioactive. But the worst
is when the immigrant becomes full
-bellied only to remain hungry for
something more complicated to attain
in a new country: respect.

Years later, I went through their life-
savings to attain a college degree—it
did not protect me: my husband and I
woke to an empty refrigerator one
day before the next day's paycheck.
We were lucky; we could have used
a credit card we were fortunate to have.
But he was mindful of beginning to
carry credit card debt; he anticipated
that small card was the wrong step
on a very slippery slope that'd already
taken down many of our hungry peers.

We got luckier. In the darkest of depths
of the cupboard lurked one more can
of tuna we swiftly opened and salted
and mayo-ed for dinner: tuna salad!
Visit me any day since and there always

พวกเขาด้วยทุ่นกระป๋องที่ซ่อนอยู่สักที่
ในบ้านอีกเป็นไหล- เป็นกำแพงด้านสุดท้าย
ป้องกันการเจมตีใดๆ ที่ไม่คาดฝัน หรือรู้ล่วงหน้าก็ตาม
เราบริจาคอาหารให้กับธนาคารอาหารทุกปี
เพื่อไม่ให้มันหมดอายุเสียก่อน
ขณะเดียวกันเราก็คอยเติมคลังเสบียง ~~ทหาร~~ อันมีค่า

แล้ว Covid-19 ก็ระบาด เราเตรียมตัวไว้แล้ว
แต่ภาวนาว่าผู้รุกรานนี้จะไม่ทำลาย
คลังเสบียงของ ~~ทหาร~~ เรา ขอให้(นักรบ)แนวหน้า
ที่ร้านขายของชำอยู่รอด และขอให้
สงครามนี้สิ้นสุด(โดยเร็ว) ในเร็ววัน เร็วคืน ...

lurk a dozen cans of tuna somewhere
in the house—a last wall of defense
against any attack, unforeseen or not.
To avoid its expiry dates, we donate
them every year to a food bank while
we replenish our valued ~~soldiers~~ stock.

Then Covid-19. We were prepared
but hoping the enemy doesn't vanquish
our ~~warriors~~ stock. May the frontliners
at the grocery stores survive and may
this battle end soon, end soon, end soon …

**ของที่ปกติไม่ซื้อ,
เรียกอีกชื่อหนึ่งว่า ชีวิตแม่บ้าน 2020**

-น้ำโซดาขวด 6 กล่อง ไม่ใช่แค่หนึ่ง-กล่องหนึ่งมี 4 ขวด

-ครีมเทียม 4 ขวด ไม่ใช่แค่หนึ่ง

-ไทโลซินของหมาที่บ้าน 12 ขวด ไม่ใช่แค่หนึ่ง

-ซอสมะเขือเทศกระป๋อง 3 กล่อง ไม่ใช่แค่สี่-กล่องหนึ่งมี 12 กระป๋อง

-เส้นสปาเกตตี 24 ห่อ ไม่ใช่แค่สี่

-ทูน่า 24 กระป๋อง ไม่ใช่แค่หก

-ซี่โครงย่างแช่แข็ง 6 ชิ้น ไม่ใช่แค่หนึ่ง

-ไก่แช่แข็ง 6 ตัว ไม่ใช่แค่หนึ่ง

-ไส้กรอกแช่แข็ง 2 โหล ไม่ใช่แค่สองชิ้น

-ตู้แช่ใหม่ขนาดใหญ่พิเศษ

-ถุงซีลสุญญากาศ 5 กล่อง ไม่ใช่แค่หนึ่ง- กล่องหนึ่งมี 5 ถุง

-โดนดูถูก 19 ครั้ง ไม่ใช่แค่สาม ในหนึ่งสัปดาห์

-.....

สำหรับทายาทของ LaSmockie Fountain

What I Normally Would Not Buy
Aka Domesticity, 2020

—6 cases, not one, of bottled seltzer water—4 bottles per case

—4 bottles, not one, of coffee creamer

—a dozen, not one, jars of Tylosin medicine for our pet dog

—3 cases, not four cans, of canned tomato sauce—12 cans per case

—24, not four, packages of spaghetti pasta

—24, not six, cans of tuna

—6, not one, rib roasts for the freezer

—6, not one, whole chickens for the freezer

—2 dozen, not two, sausages for the freezer

—a new and extra freezer

—5, not one, boxes of vacuum bags—5 bags per box

—19, not three, insults in one week

— ...

For the descendants of LaSmockie Fountain

ไม่ใช่มาสก์แรกที่เคยใส่ หรือเรียกอีกชื่อหนึ่งว่า เซลฟี่ 2020

- หลังได้อ่านข้อความ "เผื่อการระบาด 2 ชนิดสำหรับคนอเมริกันเชื้อสายเอเชียนคือ โรค Covid-19 และโรคคลั่งเชื้อชาติในชีวิตประจำวัน" โดย Brittany Wong, Huffington Post, วันที่ 26 มีนาคม 2563

ฉันไม่ได้สวมมาสก์

เพราะไวรัส แต่ฉันสวมมาสก์

เพราะพวกเขาโจมตีฉัน

ด้วยความเป็น "คนเอเชีย"

Not My First Mask aka 2020 Selfie
—after "For Asian Americans, There Are Two Pandemics: COVID-19 and Daily Bigotry" by Brittany Wong, Huffington Post, *March 26, 2020*

I don't wear a mask

because of a virus—I wear masks

because they charge me

with "Asian"

เอเชียนผู้ตื่นตระหนก
— มีนาคม 2563, สหรัฐอเมริกา

ขวดโหล
มะพร้าวกะทิเชื่อม
หนึ่งโหล

มะม่วงแผ่น
อบแห้ง
20 ห่อ

มันวุ้นย้อมผม
ให้เป็นสีบลอนด์
เทป

ติดตาสองชั้น
ปลอกถุงสวม
พยุงข้อเท้า

แก๊สกระป๋อง 15 กระป๋อง
อาหารเสบียง 100 ห่อ
และ

สตูว์ผักอบแห้ง
8 ถัง
ขนาดใหญ่

อายุการเก็บรักษา
25 ปี
ซึ่งนำมา

อุ่นกินได้ทันที
ในน้ำร้อน
จนเดือด

16

Sudden Asian Prepper
    —March 2020, U.S.A.

A dozen jars
of macapuno
preserves,

20 bags of
dried mango
jerkies,

dye for turning
hair blonde,
tape

for double-lidding eyes,
an ankle
sheath,

15 propane cans,
100 MREs,
then

8 large buckets
of vegetable
stews

with 25-year shelf
lives that
become

revived by water
if blisteringly
hot

ศรัทธาในภาวะโคโรนา
"เสบียงอาหารสำเร็จรูป" หรือที่เรียกสั้น ๆ ว่า "MRE"
คืออาหารเสบียงสำหรับหนึ่งคนโดยทำเป็นบรรจุภัณฑ์ที่มีน้ำหนักเบานำเข้า
มาโดยกระทรวงกลาโหมสหรัฐสำหรับทหารไว้ใช้ยามสงคราม...
- วิกิพีเดีย

ประธานาธิบดีแถลงการณ์
- ไม่มีอะไร เราเอาอยู่!-
วันหน้าต้องดีกว่านี้
เราจะกลับมายืนหยัด
อย่างมั่นคงกว่าเดิม!

ฉันสนองรับด้วยความศรัทธา

ด้วยข้าวของที่ฉันไม่เคยพบเจอมาก่อน:
อาหารเสบียง 100 ห่อ

ประสาทรับรสของฉันปฏิเสธมัน-

แต่เจเรมีและแอชลีย์จาก "MBF Off Grid"
บนยูทูบกดถ่านฉันกลับขณะนำเสนอ
เมนูจำกัดของอาหารเสบียงของแคนาดาคลิปที่ 2:
    มันฝรั่งอบชีสและแฮม
    แซนวิชถั่วและแยม
    ถั่วหลากชนิดกับผลไม้แห้ง
    ข้าวโอ๊ต กาแฟนมยี่ห้อเนสกาแฟ
    แอปเปิลฝาน และ "ลูกอมมินต์แก้ท้องผูก"

"กลิ่นอาจจะดูเหมือนอาหารมื้อเย็นธรรมดา
แต่รับรองว่ารสชาติดีแน่ ๆ" เจเรมีกล่าว
"เจ๋งไปเลย!" แอชลีย์ตัดสิน "ฉันให้เลย 8 เต็ม 10!"

ฉันทึ่งกับวัฒนธรรมทหาร
ในการนำเสนอลูกอมมินต์ที่ไว้กินหลังมื้ออาหาร

เจเรมีทหารเก่าพูดกลั้วหัวเราะ "ไม่ใช่แค่ลูกอมมิ้นต์สักหน่อย!
ถ้าโปรยน้ำร้อนลงไป มันจะขยายตัว

Faith in the Time of the Coronavirus

> *The "Meal, Ready to Eat"—commonly known as
> the "MRE"—is a self-contained, individual field ration in
> lightweight packaging bought by the United States
> Department of Defense for its service members for use in
> combat...*
> *—Wikipedia*

The President proclaims
        —nay, guarantees!—
BETTER DAYS AHEAD!
WE SHALL BOUNCE BACK
HIGHER THAN BEFORE!

I respond faithfully

with an item I've never experienced:
a box of 100 MREs.

My tastebuds cringe—

but Jeremy and Ashley of "MBF Off Grid"
on YouTube chide me as they
present Canada's MRE Menu #2:
        scalloped potatoes and ham,
        peanut butter and jelly sandwich,
        trail mix of nuts and dried fruits,
        oatmeal, Nescafe creamy coffee,
        sliced apples, and a "constipation mint."

"It's got that typical rationed supper food
smell but definitely tastes all right," says Jeremy.
"Awesome!" Ashley judges. "I'd give 8 out of 10!"

I marvel at the military's civility
in providing an after-dinner mint.

Ex-military Jeremy chuckles. "Not a mint!
Sprinkle with hot water and it expands

กลายเป็นผ้าเช็ดปากเลยนะ!"
ผ้าเช็ดปูก ไม่ใช่ลูกอมมิ้นท์-อะไร ๆ ไม่ได้เป็น
อย่างที่เห็นเสมอ โรงเดิม ๆ นนละ

และระบบทางสังคมที่เหมาะเจาะ
ของนักธุรกิจที่ขาดทุน
ในภาวะเศรษฐกิจตกต่ำ

ฉันสนองรับด้วยศรัทธาตามสมควร
โดยการเพิ่มจำนวน
เสบียงถุงสตวผัก
ที่เก็บได้นานกว่า 25 ปี

อะไร ๆ ไม่ได้เป็นอย่างที่เห็นเสมอไป-
กาลครั้งหนึ่งนานมาแล้ว "Faith (ศรัทธา)"
มีรากศัพท์มาจากภาษาละติน "fides" และภาษาฝรั่งเศสโบราณ "feid"
มีความหมายว่า "ศรัทธา ความเชื่อ ความมั่นใจ คำสัญญา"

to become a napkin!"

A napkin, not a mint—*the thing not
being what it seems*. What an old story

and how befitting the regime
of a businessman whose equity falls
when the economy tanks.

I respond with faith, as appropriate,
augmenting my MREs with
a bucket of vegetable stew
bearing a 25-year-shelf life.
The thing not being what it seems—
once upon a time, "faith" as derived
from the Latin "fides" and old French "feid"
meant "belief, trust, confidence, pledge."

ความตาย

ฉันมองเห็น
ความตายของฉัน

และพบว่ามัน
ช่างอึกทึก

อสุรกายนั้น
แผดเสียง

"ยอมเสียเถอะ!"

Mortality

I sight
my demise

and discover
it deafening—

the bastard
blares out

"Reconcile!"

ดอกซูกินี

*ถ้าคุณรักษ์โลก โลกจะรักษ์คุณ
แสนเรียบง่ายและแต่จะเข้าใจถึงสิ่งที่คนพื้นเมืองต้องการสื่ออย่างตรงตัวได้โ
ดยไม่ต้องใช้คำเชิงอุปมา เป็นอะไรที่ฝึกฝนได้ยาก
การแยกสองสิ่งออกจากกันนั้นสุดลึกล้ำ ยากจะหยั่งถึง...
–จาก "The Fire Next Time" โดย Leny Mendoza Strobel*

"หมด ไม่เหลือเลยสักอย่าง!"
พนักงานขายป่าวร้อง,
พร้อมโบกมือไปมาอยู่ตรงชั้นวางของ
ที่ว่างเปล่าและถือเป็นส่วนหนึ่งของ
กระแสใหม่แห่งวงการเพาะชำ
ที่ได้เห็นสุดดอกเมล็ดพันธุ์
พืช ต้นไม้ ปุ๋ยหมัก และแม้แต่ปุ๋ยมูลสัตว์
หมดเกลี้ยงเพราะผู้คนทุกกตัวอยู่บ้าน
พากันหาอะไรใหม่ ๆ น่าสนใจทำ

ต้องเกิดโรคระบาดก่อน
เราถึงจะหันมาดูแล ให้ความรัก
สวนที่เราละเลยมานาน เราหันกลับ
มาให้ความสนใจสวน
ความสนใจที่เราเคยมีให้กิจกรรมสารพัน
นอกบ้านของเรามานานเป็นปี ๆ - ทัง
ไปดูหนัง ช้อปปิ้ง ดูคอนเสิร์ต
ไปโรงละคร ถูกมือเย็นทร้านอาหาร
และที่แน่ ๆ คือ สนใจเรื่องงานที่ทำงาน
สนใจแต่ทุกอย่าง ๆ ปูแล้วปูเล่า
สวนถูกทิ้งให้แห้งร้าง ดินกได้แต่
เฝ้ารอให้ความเพิกเฉยของเรา
สิ้นสุดลง

เมื่อเราเห็นสีเหลืองสลับเขียว
เมื่อเราเห็นดอกตูมอัดแน่นไปด้วยกลีบหนา
แย้มบานดูงแสงอาทิตย์
ทูมกลางใบสีเขียวซอม ฐานดอก
ที่ติดอยู่กับผลทรงกระบอกฮัด คล้ายไส้กรอก
ของฝรั่งที่กินไม่ออน เรายิ้มกว้างให้มัน
อย่างพึงพอใจ เราไห้ร้องด้วยความปิติ
"ฝักแรกของฤดูกาลออกแล้ว!" แต่พอเรา

Zucchini Blossom

> *If you take care of the Earth, the Earth will take care of you. So simple and yet to understand what the indigenous peoples meant by this in a literal, not metaphorical sense, is difficult to practice. The disconnection is profound, so deep...*
> —from "The Fire Next Time" by Leny Mendoza Strobel

"We're out of everything!"
proclaimed the store clerk
waving his hand at emptied
shelves and forming part
of a new trend of nurseries
seeing their stock of seeds,
plants, trees, mulch and even
manure depleted as the locked
-ins look for new distractions.

It required a pandemic for us
to turn our thoughts, then loving
care, to the yard whose potential
we'd long ignored. To this yard
we brought back the attention
we'd rained for years on matters
tended outside our home—from
movies to shopping to concerts
to theaters to restaurant dining
and, of course, to jobs at an office
somewhere else. For years,
the yard remained brown, the soil
waiting for our indifference to end.

When we saw yellow interrupt the
green, when we saw a thick-petaled
bud gleam like sunlight amidst
the lush green leaves, its bottom
attached to the striped, sausage-like
body of a young zucchini, we shared
smug grins. Gleefully, we announced,
"First of the season!" But when we

ฉันกลับไปจ้องหน้าจอโทรทัศน์
ทีมนักข่าวเอาแต่รายงานจำนวนผู้เสียชีวิต
เราได้แต่หวนคิดอีกครั้งว่า
อะไรที่ทำให้เรากลายมาเป็นคนทำสวน
จุดประกายให้เราหวนกลับมาเชื่อมความสัมพันธ์กับผืนดิน

เราคนหนึ่งกระซิบปลอบขวัญอีกคน
"ซูกินีฝักแรกของเรา
ยังไงก็ต้องออกผลเพิ่มอยู่แล้ว" อีกคนกระซิบกลับไป
"แต่ทำไมกันล่ะ? ตัดออกได้เลยเหรอ?"
ริมฝีปากเผยอยิ้มกลับ แสงแดดส่อง
กระทบกระจก "ก็ตัดมาแล้วจะได้งอกใหม่ไงล่ะ"

returned attention to the television screen
whose journalists kept counting the dead,
we could only consider yet again what
was required to turn us into gardeners,
to rekindle our connections to the land.

One of us whispers to console the other,
"Our first zucchini shows new growth
is always possible." The other whispers
back, "But for what? So it can get cut off?"
The reflection's lips smile. Sunlight shines
against the mirror. "So it can nourish."

เอกวิญญาณยามโควิด

*"ถ้าคุณได้พบเจอกับชัยชนะและหายนะ
และปฏิบัติต่อจอมเสแสร้งทั้งสองนั่นแบบเดียวกัน"
-จาก "IF" โดย Rudyard Kipling*

ถ้า

กระดาษชำระ
ทั่วอลมาร์ต
หมด

ไม่มีไข่เหลือ
ที่เซฟเวย์
ทีชั่นไชน์

(ร้อนขายอาหารสำเร็จรูป
ที่ตงชู่ออย่างสดใส)
ก็ไม่มี

มิยูชและบาแก๊ต
ไม่ต้อง
กังวลไป

ฉัน
ยัง
อยู่

กับเธอ เขา หล่อน
ทรานส์
มัน

พวกเขาคือพวกเรา
คุณคือ
ฉัน—

ไม่มีคำว่า
ญา
อีกต่อไป

Kapwa On Covid

> *"If you can meet with Triumph and Disaster*
> *And treat those two impostors just the same"*
> *—from "IF" by Rudyard Kipling*

IF

Walmart is out
of toilet
paper,

Safeway is out
of eggs,
Sunshine

(the cheerfully-named gourmet
deli) is
out

of brioches and
baguettes, no
need

to worry. I
am not
out

of you, he,
she, trans,
it.

They are We.
You are
I—

There is no
IF about
it.

CODA

An N+7 Translation of
"Kapwa on Covid"

By Susan M. Schultz

Kapwa On Covid

> *"If you can meet with Trombone and Discipline*
> *And treat those two imprisonments just the same"*
> —from "IF" by Rudyard Kipling

IF

Walmart is out
of tomb
parable,

Safeway is out
of egomaniacs,
Sunshine

(the cheerfully-named grace
deli) is
out

of brioches and
baguettes, no
need

to wrapper. I
am not
out

of you, he,
she, trans,
it.

They are We.
You are
I—

There is no
IF about
it.

Behind the Scenes on Translation

I've always been fascinated by translation—including what can or cannot be translated. Thus, I wanted to share some thought processes as I, Natthaya Thamdee and Susan M. Schultz considered my Covid-19 poems.

Thai Translations
Four issues came up in my discussions with Natthaya, who says

> Since translation is a conveying process of different cultures, nations, and perspectives, I encountered a cultural untranslatability, like in the poem "Poetics March 2020." For the phrase "what stains the air" in 9th stanza, I asked if she meant "the situation that just happened or literally air pollution"? Of course, the answer to this question was that it contains both metaphorical and implicature senses. In translating this phrase into Thai, I mostly couldn't use the literal translation. Free translation, where you have to truly understand the meaning and sense of the original and convert it into an understandable sense, was applied in translating poems.

For this first issue, the specific Q&A was

> **Natthaya**: The first poem, "Poetics, March 2020," 9th stanza, that says what stains the air .
> Do you mean "the situation that just happened" or literally "air pollution"?
>
> **Eileen**: It's a metaphor. So (pure) air is pure, like the beginning before things happen. What "stains" it are the events that happen, making the air dirty.
>
> That stanza is also a generalization about a poem's power to look at various events and then figure out their significance ("alchemizes into the clarity") where clarity can mean the significance or meaning of various events.

A second issue surfaced in the poem "Faith in the Time of the Coronavirus" where, as Natthaya puts it,

> the poem mentions a channel on Youtube owned by a military veteran. Well, I had no idea who he is and what that channel is about. Also, the phrase of *"the thing not being what it seems"* had been raised as a comparison of a napkin and a mint. I and my Thai editor had no clues about this at all so that I had to ask Eileen for more explanation. Yes, this is what's called a 'cultural untranslatability'.

The specific Q&A was

> **Natthaya:**
> Question please! I don't get the sense and meaning of these phrases
> > "Not a mint!
> > Sprinkle with hot water and it expands
> > To become a napkin!"
> > A napkin, not a mint—*the thing not
> > Being what it seems.*
>
> Would you please explain this to me?
>
> **Eileen:**
> So this is a way of saying that things are not necessarily what they look like or what they seem to be. Like, what looks like tiny mint candy is actually a ball of paper that can expand to a napkin when the ball is sprinkled with water. Mint candy is raised here as some people use mint candy to refresh their breaths after eating a meal.
>
> "The thing not being what it seems" is a particular phrase known in some circles, which is why I worded it like that.
>
> Given the poem's theme of "faith," sometimes one believes in something even though it's not evident that that belief is warranted. A metaphor again :). Like, simplistically, believing that the ball is a napkin even though it looks like something else (mint candy).
> Hope that helps!

A third issue came up in the poem "Kapwa on Covid" in terms of incorporating the hay(na)ku form. The English poem uses the reverse hay(na)ku form of tercets where the first line consists of three words, the second line of two words, and the third line of one word. I allowed the Thai version to elide the hay(na)ku form after the following discussion based on the poem's first stanza

> Walmart is out
> of toilet
> paper.

The hay(na)ku form did not translate to Thai where Natthaya's translation is

> กระดาษชำระ
>
> ที่วอลมาร์ต
>
> หมด

which literally translates in Thai as "Toilet paper / at Walmart / is out,". Natthaya says she could have translated literally my English "Walmart is out/ of toilet / paper" but it would be unnatural to state it as such in Thai. Also, word-count is a challenge when there are differences in how language can be omissive; for example, Natthaya explains, "The English phrase of 'She is beautiful' would be translated to the Thai 'เธอสวย' or 'She-beautiful'."

No doubt this literal versus conceptual balance exists in all types of language translations but, in this case, the Thai could not support the hay(na)ku form if one were to use more authentic Thai speech. I let the matter go because this issue reminded me—and I am suddenly beset by guilt over—when I once asked some Romanian translators to re-do their translation of some of my hay(na)ku poems to abide by the 1-2-3 form constraint. Since I am not fluent in Romanian, I can't judge whether their reformatted translations were/are effective. But I now wonder whether I shouldn't have been pleased at seeing how the Romanian words abide by the hay(na)ku word count. As Natthaya points out for Thai, language that's artificially constrained might be … artificial. C'est la vie.

Our fourth and last issue revolved around translating <u>the title INCULPATORY EVIDENCE</u>. Here's our original Q&A:

> **Natthaya:**
> **INCULPATORY EVIDENCE** is evidence that shows, or tends to show, a person's involvement in an act, or evidence that can establish guilt. It literally means "หลักฐานเชิงประจักษ์" (luk-tan-cherng-pra-chak) in Thai.
>
> หลักฐาน (luk-tan) is an evidence.
> เชิงประจักษ์ (cherng-pra-chak) is empirical.
>
> For the translation, I want to maintain the sense of original as much as possible.
> So, I keep the "INCULPATORY" as literally translated, but I interpreted "EVIDENCE" in your title as "disaster."
>
> So, the Thai translation is **"หายนะเชิงประจักษ์"** (hai-ya-na-cherng-pra-chak) or literally means "INCULPATORY DISASTER" which I think is attractive, dark, and interesting. What do you think?
>
> **INCULPATORY EVIDENCE**
> **หายนะเชิงประจักษ์**
>
> **The Covid-19 Poems**
> **บทกวี Covid-19**

> **Eileen:**
> Dear Natthaya,
Thank you for these. As regards the title, based on your explanation I think I would prefer for "evidence" to be translated

as "evidence" rather than the "disaster" version. This relates to how I wish the reader to be the one to conclude "disaster" rather than me saying so didactically to the reader. I present the poems as evidence and then the readers (not me) would be the one to interpret them. Does that make sense, or address your thought process?

> **Natthaya**
> Oh, ok. I forgot that. I interpreted it as a reader of your poems. Now, I understand. Thank you. Evidence sounds better. Your poems are really an evidence!!
>
> So, the title would be หลักฐานเชิงประจักษ์. A literal interpretation for *INCULPATORY EVIDENCE*.

Natthaya later (graciously) added, "*INCULPATORY EVIDENCE*—actually, this title clarifies as soon as I re-read it. From the first poem until the last one, all are included in this title, in my view as a reader and translator. The poems touch me even deeply when they were converted into Thai, especially the last poem 'Kapwa On Covid'."

*

Oulipian N+7

My discussions with Natthaya touched on how translations can fail, albeit acceptably. This issue also occurred when I sent the poems over to another poet, Susan M. Schultz for her possible feedback—including perhaps undergoing the Oulipian n+7 process in which she'd been working for years. In its guide to OULIPO, Poets.org explains

> Although poetry and mathematics often seem to be incompatible areas of study, the philosophy of OULIPO seeks to connect them. Founded in 1960 by French mathematician Francois de Lionnais and writer Raymond Queneau, *Ouvroir de Litterature Potentielle* (OULIPO), or Workshop of Potential Literature, investigates the possibilities of verse written under a system of structural

constraints. Lionnais and Quenuau believed in the profound potential of a poem produced within a framework or formula and that, if done in a playful posture, the outcomes could be endless.

One of the most popular OULIPO formulas is "N+7," in which the writer takes a poem already in existence and substitutes each of the poem's substantive nouns with the noun appearing seven nouns away in the dictionary. Care is taken to ensure that the substitution is not just a compound derivative of the original, or shares a similar root, but a wholly different word. Results can vary widely depending on the version of the dictionary one uses.

Susan has been doing Oulipian n+7s of political language since at least 2012, when she ran Mitt Romney's words through the generator. Since 2016, she's also "translated" Trump's tweets. A 50-page collection of them was published by Dispatches from the Poetry Wars and featured at https://www.dispatchespoetrywars.com/virtual-chapbooks/the-viewpoint-is-presumption/.

Susan says, "I have found that n+7 works best as parody, rather than as straight translation. Using this method, I usually take language that I find absurd and make it even more absurd. Sometimes it moves from terrifying to funny, with that layer of terror still somehow apparent to the reader or listener."

Against that backdrop, Susan notes,

> When Eileen sent me her Covid poems, I wondered if that technique was appropriate. After all, this is a serious time. People are in pain, Eileen's poems are serious and ethical. What to do. But the poem based on Rudyard Kipling ("Kapwa on Covid") offers an opening. The poem begins with a list of consumer items, including toilet paper, that were hoarded when the pandemic began. It's a story of consumerism mixed horribly with illness, disease, and fear. That part of the poem lends itself to parody. Toward the end, when Eileen is making an argument that we are all

> linked in a profound way (via pronouns here) the poem
> refuses to be translated. As it should be. Thank you, Eileen!

The poem refuses to be translated. As it should be. Au contraire, Susan! I thank you for affirming the nature of poetry and ensuring my poems remained … poems!

I've been blessed to collaborate with Natthaya Thamdee and Susan M. Schultz to create *INCUPATORY EVIDENCE*. I hope this look behind the (translation) scenes is also interesting to you, Dear Reader. Thank you, Universe.

—Eileen R. Tabios
July 2020

Afterword: some thoughts, 01 June 2020, which may well be obsolete by the time you read this. And which may very well seem quaint to Eileen's readers from the far distant future.

By John Bloomberg-Rissman

1.
The first reported case of COVID-19 (the name of the disease caused by the novel coronavirus, SARS-CoV-2, short for "Coronavirus Disease 2019") is perhaps that of a 55-year-old individual from Hubei province, China, Nov. 17, 2019. But of course, no one knows for sure. In any case, by Jan 2, 2020, 41 admitted hospital patients, all in Wuhan (Hubei province), had been laboratory-confirmed as having the disease. Fast-forward to 24 May, which is when I begin this writing: there are now close to 5.5 million confirmed cases worldwide, and close to 350,000 deaths. COVID-19 has been confirmed in at least 213 countries and territories. We are in the midst of a pandemic, which is completely out of control.

2.
There is no treatment at present for COVID-19. The only strategies that have had any effect have been self-isolation and social distancing when isolation has been impossible. The purpose of these strategies is to "flatten the curve," as the expression has it, which means to slow the spread of the disease so as not to overwhelm health services, that's all. Not to eradicate the danger of contagion—that isn't why these strategies were developed.

3.
China began to lock down everyone in Hubei province except those in essential industries in late January. Most of the rest of the world slowly followed. Other countries in Asia began to lock down shortly after China. Italy locked down in late February, but the rest of Europe didn't lock down until March. The Americas began to lock down around mid-March. Sub-Saharan Africa began to lock down a week or so later than did the Americas.

4.
The United States waited more than three months from the first reported case to begin to lock down, and it did so in a patchwork manner, state by state, and to differing degrees everywhere. The US only gets special mention here because its special level of incompetence has made it, as of this writing, far and away the world's leader in number of cases reported (almost 1.7 million), and number of deaths (there will be 100, 000 by tonight or tomorrow).

5.
The lockdowns worked. In many parts of the world the curve did indeed slightly flatten.

6.
Oh, and did I mention that many nurses are facing pay cuts?

7.
Actually, I lied a bit in 4. There are other reasons the US gets special mention. First, because both Eileen and I live in the US (she in northern and I in southern California). Second, because, in two months, the leadership of the US, from the federal down to the state and local level, and an unbelievable number of the inhabitants of this country (millions upon millions of them), have forgotten WHY we locked down, and have decided that there's no more reason for the lockdown, and that it's over. Two months in not a long time. But, apparently, it's too long for too many USAmericans to keep the reason why we "flattened the curve" in their thoughts.

8.
To be fair to the US, many other countries have also begun to re-open. Their leadership, inhabitants, etc, seem to have become amnesiac as well.

9.
To be fair, there are other reasons people worldwide want the lockdown to end besides amnesia. There are strong economic incentives for reopening. Many people have had no sources of income. Many businesses have had no sources of revenue. The

entire system of world capitalism has been under a great deal of stress.

10.
But there are reasons to put the emphasis on amnesia. For one, and this is true worldwide, many people have not gone straight back to work. They have gone straight to the beach, to bars, to restaurants, to churches, to shops ... they have in fact used the early days of re-opening to participate in almost every other sort of activity than those that affect their own economic interests.

11.
One of the things people have been told to do in many parts of the US is to wear masks when going outside. Most masks are not medical grade. They are designed to keep people from sneezing and coughing on each other. This common and painless courtesy has not had the intended effect. Many have refused to wear masks. Many have gone out of their way to spit or cough upon mask-wearers. At least one person has died because she was spit on by an infected person. She was doing nothing to that person. She was not even interacting with them. Some shops have refused entrance to mask wearers.

12.
It is probably true that the number of such blatantly sociopathic incidents is small when compared to the total number of human interactions. But it is also true that the amount of time spent so far in non-work-related activities is a lot.

13.
It's not just amnesia. I should also put the emphasis on immaturity, hostility, and selfishness. At least in the US. I do not know whether precisely this same syndrome is taking place in other countries. Though I do know that in many places people have been cited or arrested for breaking lockdown. Stories emanated out of China that the doors and windows of some apartment buildings had to be boarded up to keep people in.

14.
One important fact is that suffering (including death rates) varies among populations, by both class and race or ethnicity. It shouldn't be necessary to say that the poor and the dark are suffering disproportionally, because they always are. This sad fact has been and continues to be true everywhere.

15.
And it isn't just health outcomes that are at issue or on display here. To quote a CBS news report from just yesterday, "A sign displayed at a McDonald's in Guangzhou, China, read 'black people are not allowed to enter'—just one instance of a growing problem in the city. Discrimination based on efforts to contain the coronavirus in China have sparked an outcry in Africa and other places around the world, as the U.S. grapples with its own spike in discrimination against Asians over fears of the disease. Photos and videos out of Guangzhou show police detaining Africans over concern they could be spreading the coronavirus, CBS News' Ramy Inocencio reports. Images of Africans sleeping on the street after being evicted from their homes have also incited backlash." Chinese people have faced hostility and physical violence in Europe and Asian-Americans of many national backgrounds have been under attack in the US. On April 21st, *Vox* reported that "According to Stop AAPI Hate, an organization that's been tracking self-reported incidents, more than 1,100 physical and verbal attacks against Asian Americans have been documented since late March." During that period Donald Trump and Mike Pompeo persisted in using terms like "Chinese virus" and "Wuhan virus", which undoubtedly contributed to that.

16.
Unsurprisingly, during the lockdown, because the abused have been trapped inside with their abusers, there has been an uptick in the already horrific number of victims of domestic violence.

17.
Meanwhile, back on the global warming front, in spite of the lockdowns that reduced traffic, flying, and other sources of emissions, CO2 levels continue to rise. According to the Earth System Research Laboratories Global Monitoring Lab, which is part of the US government's NOAA, April 2020 CO2 levels stood at 416.21 ppm. Compare that to those of April 2019: 413.33 ppm. So there's no good news on that front.

18.
While we're talking about the environment, I would be remiss not to mention that, according to a *Guardian* article of May 11, "During the Covid-19 lockdown, US federal agencies have eased fuel-efficiency standards for new cars; frozen rules for soot air pollution; proposed to drop review requirements for liquefied natural gas terminals; continued to lease public property to oil and gas companies; sought to speed up permitting for offshore fish farms; and advanced a proposal on mercury pollution from power plants that could make it easier for the government to conclude regulations are too costly to justify their benefits. The government has also relaxed reporting rules for polluters during the pandemic."

19.
During the first half of 2020, in the midst of the pandemic, the US has been considering the first nuclear bomb test since 1992, and North Korea has announced that it is beefing up its nuclear arsenal.

20.
While we're talking about war and rumors of war, Trump has announced that the US is pulling out of the Open Skies agreement, which has 30 signatories. The 1992 treaty allows member countries to conduct short-notice, unarmed, reconnaissance flights over the other countries to collect data on their military forces and activities. It is the latest major arms control treaty that the US will abandon under the Trump administration. The administration claim is that Russia has been in consistent violation of this treaty, and that such a withdrawal will force

Putin and company to reconsider. True or not, that's one more safeguard down.

20a.
This was written before the police murder of George Floyd and the worldwide reaction to it, which, as of mid-June 2020, is ongoing, just like the pandemic, just like CO_2 emissions, just like domestic abuse, just like everything.

21.
I could go on and on. Anyone could. I'll let the keepers of the Doomsday Clock sum it up: "Humanity continues to face two simultaneous existential dangers — nuclear war and climate change — that are compounded by a threat multiplier, cyber-enabled information warfare, that undercuts society's ability to respond. The international security situation is dire, not just because these threats exist, but because world leaders have allowed the international political infrastructure for managing them to erode ... As seasoned watchers know, the Doomsday Clock did not move in 2019. But the Clock's minute hand was set forward in January 2018 by 30 seconds, to two minutes before midnight, the closest it had been to midnight since 1953 in the early years of the Cold War. Previously, the Clock was moved from three minutes to midnight to two and a half minutes to midnight in January 2017. This year [2020], the Science and Security Board moved the time from two minutes to 100 seconds to midnight, a decision taken in full recognition of its historic nature." That last phrase means it is (we are) closer to midnight than it has ever been (than we have ever been).

22.
This is the background against which I read Eileen's poems.

23.
So when I get to the lines in "Poetics, March 2020" that read:

>   Photographs
>   reveal that the image of a dried tear

> shows similar passages of erosion
>
> as have etched earth for years. "Amazing
> how the patterns of nature seem so
> similar, regardless of scale," notes
>
> the photographer Rose-Lynn Fisher. Anguish
> begets the same images of branched crystals
> whether from dried tears that formed
>
> in moments or from the consistent deterioration
> of a terrain over prolonged passages of time
> "As though each tear is a microcosm of
>
> collective human experience, like one drop
> of an ocean," says Fisher

I wonder to myself why my utter certainty, confirmed by behaviors evident during the pandemic, that humanity in simply incapable of making its way of out the hole(s) it has dug for itself elicits no tears from me, while at the same time I am moved by landscapes scored by rivers and their tributaries, I am moved by the similar patterns I find etched into the bark of trees (have I mentioned the Sixth Extinction event yet?) ... why no tears? Perhaps the planet of which I am a part is doing my crying for me? I don't know.

24.
And when I read "Regret", the lines

> As plastic bags return
> the fish are simply shivering—
>
> their fear roils the water
> and overcomes shores with
>
> turbulent tears

I think that perhaps I am right, I need not cry because all there are, are tears. A planet that at present is made of tears.

25.
But when I read "NOT MY FIRST MASK aka 2020 SELFIE"

>I don't wear a mask

>because of a virus—I wear masks

>because they charge me

>with "Asian"

I begin to realize why I have no tears. It's because I am tired. I am tired of planetary destruction. I am tired of human-upon human destruction (xenophobia and racism are forms of destruction). I am tired living among a species that goes amnesiac within two months. I am so tired. I am so fucking tired I ... well, let's just leave it at that.

26.
When I read "Sudden Asian Prepper" I had to write Eileen and ask her if

>tape

>for double-lidding eyes

was a real thing. She assured me it was. I found YouTube videos explaining how it works. Now I am even more exhausted.

27.
"Faith in the Time of the Coronavirus" opens with the lines

>The President proclaims
>>—nay, guarantees!—
>*BETTER DAYS AHEAD!*

*WE SHALL BOUNCE BACK
HIGHER THAN BEFORE!*

I suppose that, technically, the president is a narcissist. OK. That explains a lot. But what explains this? When Trump was elected his approval rating was approximately 42%. Three and a half years later his approval rating is within a few tenths of a percent of that. It doesn't matter what the man does. People who love him will love him, even if he gets them killed, they will worship him from the beyond. I can only come up with one explanation: 40-something percent of the US population is a danger to everything else that breathes and lives. Given the concurrent rise to power of Trump-like people on every continent I think it is reasonably safe to generalize that statistic to the entire human population of the earth. I could use other descriptors, but let's stick with dangerous. At the end of this afterword I'm going to come back to that.

28.
The same poem goes on to note

> I respond faithfully
>
> with an item I've never experienced:
> a box of 100 MREs.

Just because I don't seem to have any tears left doesn't mean I can't laugh. At the outset of this pandemic my brother told me that he had a box of MRE's in his garage. "You know what the irony is?" he asked. "They are mostly carbs. And I'm a diabetic." That's what passes for funny around here.

29.
I want to quote "Mortality" in full:

> I sight
> my demise
>
>
> and discover

it deafening—

the bastard
blares out

"Reconcile!"

I totally get that. At first, when this pandemic started, I thought, "Well, now I know what is going to kill me." I'm in one of the particularly vulnerable categories—"An aged man is but a paltry thing, / A tattered coat upon a stick"* etc. For about two days I was a little hysterical. So I thought, well, that's no good. Since I am mortal, whether or not it's the virus that gets me I'd better get right with that 100% inescapable fact. So my wife and I turned an hour or two a day of this lockdown into a meditation retreat. I hope it's working. I'll try to remember to let you know when the time comes.

(*WB Yeats, "Sailing to Byzantium")

30.
"Kapwa On Covid" ends with the lines

>I
>am not
>out
>
>of you, he,
>she, trans,
>it.
>
>They are We.
>You are
>I—
>
>There is no
>IF about
>it.

Not one word I've written here is to be taken in any way contrary to this.

31.
The thing is. The thing is, I now realize beyond the least shadow of a doubt, that we are fucked. We are fucked because of what we are. Too many of us are dangerous. Too many of us have always been dangerous. We are a somewhat lovely species, but we will not rise to the challenges that face us. We have failed, we have always failed, we will continue to fail. And we have yet to fail better. We just fail. In terms of long-term survival, a species that cannot remember what it was doing for a mere two months does not have much going for it. Maybe that's why I don't have any more tears. Because I can see that so clearly now. I am so tired.

32.
Given my exhaustion and hopelessness, why do I bother to write this, to append it to Eileen's book? Why am I happy to see her book published? Why am I happy to see that it has been translated into another language?

33.
I write this because I know I am not alone with my fears, and in my exhaustion. Among many other signs, Eileen's poems reveal that. Among many other signs, the fact that someone wants to translate her words reveals that. It's not particularly important to me that the translation is into Thai, though that's lovely. It could be into any language. It could be into a number of languages simultaneously, like a polyglot bible. Perhaps it should be. Translation, at its root, is an act of "carrying across." From one, place, or language, or person, to another. Translation, like poetry, like music, is a shared activity. Did you know that the eight musicians who played for the passengers of the Titanic as the ship went down were from two separate groups? I didn't. That night, they played together. That's enough. "Let there be songs / to fill the air."

Selected Notes on the Poems

Faith in the Time of the Coronavirus
Written after a YouTube episode of "MBF Off Grid" (Feb. 2, 2020): https://www.youtube.com/watch?v=LU89jT4MQMU

Kapwa On Covid
Written after YouTube video of Michael Caine reading "IF" by Rudyard Kipling. "Kapwa," as articulated by Dr. Katrin de Guia, "reflects a viewpoint that beholds the essential humanity recognizable in everyone, therefore linking (including) people rather than separating (excluding) them from each other" ("Roots of Filipino Humanism" by Karina Lagdameo-Santillan, *pressenza International Press Agency*, July 24, 2018). The poem is written in the reverse hay(na)ku form (more information on the hay(na)ku at https://eileenrtabios.com/haynaku/).

Poetics, March 2020
References to Rose-Lynn Fisher come from "The Microscopic Structures of Dried Human Tears" by Joseph Stromberg, *Smithsonian Magazine*, Nov. 19, 2013
https://www.smithsonianmag.com/science-nature/the-microscopic-structures-of-dried-human-tears-180947766/

Sudden Asian Prepper
The poem is written in the reverse hay(na)ku form (more information on the hay(na)ku at https://eileenrtabios.com/haynaku/)

What I Normally Would Not Buy / *Aka Domesticity, 2020*
The poem is written after "Domestic violence increased during coronavirus lockdowns," *The Economist,* April 22, 2020. LaSmockie Fountain was a victim of domestic violence in 1995. Marking the fifth anniversary of her death, her aunt Sharon Stafford called her "such a lovely person, very beautiful, a great mother, and she absolutely loved to dance." (*13Maz.com*, May 24, 2020)

About the Poets & Translators

Eileen R. Tabios has released about 60 collections of poetry, fiction, essays, and experimental biographies from publishers in ten countries and cyberspace. *INCULPATORY EVIDENCE* is her third bilingual edition. Recent releases include a short story collection, *PAGPAG: The Dictator's Aftermath in the Diaspora* and a poetry collection, *The In(ter)vention of the Hay(na)ku: Selected Tercets 1996-2019.* Her award-winning body of work includes invention of the hay(na)ku, a 21st century diasporic poetic form, as well as a first poetry book, *Beyond Life Sentences*, which received the Philippines' National Book Award for Poetry. Translated into 11 languages, she also has edited, co-edited or conceptualized 15 anthologies of poetry, fiction and essays. Her writing and editing works have received recognition through awards, grants and residencies. More information is available at http://eileenrtabios.com

Natthaya Thamdee has been working as a freelance translator since 2011 when she began her master's study, majoring in translation studies, at Mahidol University. Her first job was to translate subtitles of movies and TV programs from English into Thai. She then focused her master's thesis on translating Thai folk songs into English which contained prosodies, rhymes, and cultural senses. She shares, "People kept saying why about my thesis and my advisor said about my thesis that it was 'hyper-active or mad thesis'. The answer is that there is something very appealing in poetry and the challenge to interpret keeps me interested in translating poetry until today." Currently, she works as a lecturer at Vongchavalitkul University, in its Languages department, while continuing to work as a freelance translator for jobs that match her interest, such as translating *Inculpatory Evidence.*

John Bloomberg-Rissman is an editor and mashup ethnographer slash maker of texts. Among other projects, he has co-edited one volume of the series *Poems for the Millennium* and a two-volume anthology called *The End of the World Project*, as well as currently co-editing *The Collected Poems and Verse Translations* *of Anselm Hollo*. His own work is ongoing and has been for about 15 years. It's called *Zeitgeist Spam*, of which three sections have been published; the fourth is currently in progress. He is aging-in-place in San Diego, California.

Susan M. Schultz is the author of many books of poetry and poetic prose, most recently *I Want to Write an Honest Sentence* from Talisman House, which is a close relative to her life-long project, *Memory Cards*. She has lived in Hawai`i since 1990. She founded Tinfish Press in 1990 and was Editor until 2019.

www.ingramcontent.com/pod-product-compliance
Lightning Source LLC
Chambersburg PA
CBHW071242090426
42736CB00014B/3181